Pooped Puppies

Published by Sellers Publishing, Inc.

161 John Roberts Road, South Portland, ME 04106
Visit us at www.sellerspublishing.com • E-mail: rsp@rsvp.com

Copyright © 2015 Sellers Publishing, Inc.
All rights reserved.

Compiled by Robin Haywood

ISBN: 978-1-4162-4570-4

Printed and bound in China.

Cover image © 2015 LEDA
Credits appear on page 128.

10 9 8 7 6 5 4 3 2 1

Pooped Puppies

life's too short to work like a dog

SELLERS

PUBLISHING

Work is the refuge
of people who have
nothing better to do.

Oscar Wilde

I always arrive
late at the office,
but I make
up for it by
leaving early.

Charles Lamb

Work is not always
required. There is such a
thing as sacred idleness.

George MacDonald

We need quiet time to examine our lives openly and honestly . . . spending quiet time alone gives your mind an opportunity to renew itself and create order.

Susan L. Taylor

11

I slip from workaholic to bum real easy.

Matthew Broderick

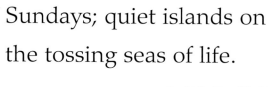

Sundays; quiet islands on
the tossing seas of life.

S. W. Duffield

I do not like work,
even when someone
else does it.

Mark Twain

Tension is who you
think you should be.
Relaxation is who
you are.

Chinese proverb

I have long been of the opinion that if work were such a splendid thing the rich would have kept more of it for themselves.

Bruce Grocott

21

I don't generally feel anything until noon; then it's time for my nap.

Bob Hope

In a dream you
are never eighty.

Anne Sexton

Think what a better world it would be if we all, the whole world, had milk and cookies about three o'clock every afternoon and then lay down on our blankets for a nap.

Barbara Jordan

Doing nothing is
very hard to do . . .
you never know
when you're finished.

Leslie Nielsen

Besides the noble art of getting things done, there is a nobler art of leaving things undone. The wisdom of life consists in the elimination of nonessentials.

Lin Yutang

Anything worth doing
is worth doing slowly.

Mae West

When the sun rises, I go to work.

When the sun goes down, I take my rest.

I dig the well from which I drink.

I farm the soil which yields

my food. I share creation.

Kings can do no more.

Chinese proverb

Whatever you can
do or dream
you can, begin it.
Boldness has
genius, power,
and magic in it.

Johann Wolfgang von Goethe

Sleeping is no mean art: for its sake one must stay awake all day.

Friedrich Nietzsche

Anything that can't be done in bed isn't worth doing at all.

Groucho Marx

Embrace simplicity,
Reduce selfishness,
Have few desires.

Lao-tzu

Nothing cures
insomnia like the
realization that it's
time to get up.

Author unknown

Learning to ignore things
is one of the great paths
to inner peace.

Robert J. Sawyer

Simple pleasures are the last refuge of the complex.

Oscar Wilde

Sometimes the most important thing in a whole day is the rest we take between two deep breaths.

Etty Hillesum

The more faithfully
you listen to the voices
within you, the better
you will hear what is
sounding outside.

Dag Hammarskjöld

Climb the mountains and get their good tidings. Nature's peace will flow into you as sunshine flows into trees. The winds will blow their own freshness into you, and the storms their energy, while cares will drop off like autumn leaves.

John Muir

Dreams are illustrations . . .
from the book your
soul is writing about you.

Marsha Norman

To sit with a dog on a hillside on a glorious afternoon is to be back in Eden, where doing nothing was not boring — it was peace.

Milan Kundera

It is better to have loafed
and lost than never to have
loafed at all.

James Thurber

I've developed a
new philosophy . . .
I only dread one day
at a time.

Charles Schulz (Charlie Brown)

The reason why
worry kills more
people than work
is that more people
worry than work.

Robert Frost

Consciousness:
that annoying time
between naps.

Author unknown

Problems always
look smaller after
a warm meal and a
good night's sleep.

Anonymous

So little time,

and so little to do.

Oscar Levant

I don't have anything against work. I just figure, why deprive somebody who really loves it.

Dobie Gillis

Dreaming permits each and every one of us to be quietly and safely insane every night of our lives.

Charles William Dement

I love sleep. My life has the tendency to fall apart when I'm awake, you know?

Ernest Hemingway

If you are losing your leisure,
look out; you may be losing
your soul.

Anonymous

No day is so bad it can't be fixed with a nap.

Carrie Snow

We spend most of our time and energy in a kind of horizontal thinking. We move along the surface of things . . . but, there are times when we must stop. We sit still. We lose ourselves in a pile of leaves or in its memory. We listen, and breezes from a whole other world begin to whisper.

James Carroll

Sometimes opportunity knocks, but most of the time it sneaks up and then quietly steals away.

Doug Larson

I try to take one day at a time, but sometimes several days attack me at once.

Jennifer Yane

The mark of a successful person is one who has spent an entire day on the bank of a river without feeling guilty about it.

Author unknown

How beautiful it is to do nothing, and then to rest afterward.

Spanish proverb

If people
concentrated
on the really
important things
in life, there'd be
a shortage of
fishing poles.

Doug Larson

If your dreams turn
to dust . . . vacuum.

Author unknown

A good rest is half the work.

Yugoslav proverb

Sitting quietly,
doing nothing,
spring comes and
the grass grows
by itself.

Zen proverb

Troubles are a lot like people —
they grow bigger if you nurse them.

Author unknown

Sometimes it's important
to work for that pot of
gold. But other times it's
essential to take time off
and to make sure that your
most important decision
in the day simply consists
of choosing which color to
slide down on the rainbow.

Douglas Pagels

Life is something that
happens when you can't
get to sleep.

Fran Lebowitz

Hold fast to dreams.

For if dreams die,

life is a broken-winged

bird that cannot fly.

James Langston Hughes

I like work; it fascinates me. I can sit and look at it for hours.

Jerome K. Jerome

At some point, you gotta
let go and sit still and allow
contentment to come to you.

Elizabeth Gilbert

The best way to appreciate your job is to imagine yourself without one.

Oscar Wilde

Cheerfulness and contentment are great beautifiers and are famous preservers of youthful looks.

Charles Dickens

A contented mind is the greatest blessing a person can enjoy in this world.

Joseph Addison

If you can dream it,
you can do it.

Walt Disney

Peace is rarely denied
to the peaceful.

Johann von Schiller

Personally, I have
nothing against work,
particularly when
performed quietly
and unobtrusively by
someone else.

Barbara Ehrenreich

Blessed is the person
who is too busy to
worry in the daytime
and too sleepy to
worry at night.

Author unknown

Work is the greatest thing in the world. So we should always save some of it for tomorrow.

Don Herold

Credits